ARMED FORCES INFORMATION AND EDUCATION • DEPARTMENT OF DEFENSE

VIETNAM

A POCKET GUIDE TO
VIETNAM

Foreword by Bruns Grayson,
Vietnam Veteran, US Army

Bodleian Library
UNIVERSITY OF OXFORD

First published by the Department of Defense, USA, 1962.
Revised edition, 1966.

We have updated the use of Vietnamese diacritics to match
modern conventions where relevant.

This edition first published in 2011 by the Bodleian Library
Broad Street
Oxford OX1 3BG

www.bodleianbookshop.co.uk

ISBN 978 1 85124 285 6

Cover design by Dot Little
Design and layout by JCS Publishing Services Ltd
in Caslon 10/12.25 and Gill Sans
Printed and bound in China by C&C Offset Printing Co. Ltd
on 100 gsm Chinese Sen Po Enlanda 1.7

British Library Catalogue in Publishing Data
A CIP record of this publication is available from
the British Library

CONTENTS

*DoD PG - 21A
*DA Pam 360 - 411
*NAVPERS 93135A
*AFP 190-4-3
*NAVMC 2593A

*Supersedes DoD PG-21/DA Pam 20-198/NAVPERS 93135/AFP
190-4-3/NAVMC 2593/6, December 1962.

Variety of vehicles spices Saigon traffic.

Farmers plant rice in Vietnam's lowlands.

FOREWORD

I must have received this handbook sometime in the spring of 1968, before heading to Vietnam that summer. I did not keep it and had not thought about it since I left the country in February 1970 and took up life outside the army. Then last year, by chance, Bodleian Library Publishing asked me to look it over, wondering, in particular, if there was any aspect of it that would be offensive or noxious to veterans. And so I read it again after forty years, and dim memories got a little sharper.

The publisher's question underlines the special place the Vietnam War has in the imagination of the West in general and the United States in particular; still a prickly and fraught topic after all these years. The war is imagined by its (few) defenders as a particularly dramatic example of noble resistance during the Cold War and imagined by its (many) opponents as either, at best, a foolish waste, or, at worst, an imperialistic, racist, and close to criminal enterprise. No one who touches any corner of the history can escape the polemical past of Vietnam. But someone seeking to make the racist and imperialist case finds little help in this handbook. The admonitions on the first page to think of one's self as a guest, to be deferential, helpful, interested, and accommodating of custom and manners speak for themselves. The descriptions of family life and the social practices of the people speak of a writer highly conversant with the actual manners of the Vietnamese, who are formal, clannish, and determined.

There is a very real question, of course, of how much force such a guidebook could have in forming the behaviour of the average American soldier—about twenty years old, not well-educated, not wily enough to avoid the draft in most cases, very often on his first trip away from the United States. I don't know what the Vietnamese equivalent of 'overpaid, oversexed and over here' was, but there must have been one, and such a phrase would have described almost all of us. We were curious, scared, open, friendly, and preoccupied with how much time we had left before we could go home. We were no more loutish and noisy than any similar collection of young innocents would be, but certainly no less.

What the handbook could not convey to any of us is how alien the culture would feel to such American ingénues. Saigon, it is true, had and has lovely French colonial architecture but it also had in those days very large squatters' villages where people lived in shacks constructed entirely from flattened beer cans. The city reeked of raw sewage and unfamiliar cooking smells. Thousands of motorbikes buzzed incessantly and seemed to move randomly but somehow avoided, for the most part, being crushed under the wheels of big trucks and armoured vehicles travelling the same roads. Something as ordinary as the sight of Vietnamese soldiers holding hands as they walked four or five abreast brought us up short the first few times we saw it. The sounds of spoken Vietnamese, too, could not be conveyed on the written page. There is a nasal, sing-song quality to the language that is grating to an untuned ear. The word 'ba' could mean half a dozen different things, depending on subtle falls or rises in tone that we simply could not hear. Unless you were exhaustively trained in language school or were a linguistic prodigy (or happened to speak French, which was fairly common among the Vietnamese) you resorted to a rough patois of English, French, and Vietnamese useful only for the most primitive conversations.

We employed the same patois with one another, slipping butchered Vietnamese and French into everyday speech with military jargon and slang thrown in for good measure: 'We gotta di di five clicks to firebase Yankee Zulu and there's beaucoup hostiles sighted.' That was our everyday talk, mostly accompanied by words not fit for publication.

There is a good deal of historical and cultural information packed into this little book, and a political point of view more or less assumed: we would be fighting to preserve freedom and to prevent the spread of a pernicious idea, communism. It is interesting that the booklet accurately and briefly describes the history of the Vietnamese resisting outsiders—the Chinese and others— while assuming that we could never be cast in such a light.

The North Vietnamese understood the temperament of their people and skilfully employed that sense of nationalism to mobilize them. They were also implacable. Early in the hotter part of the war there was an engagement between North Vietnamese regulars and the First Air Cavalry Division. It took place over three days in the central highlands and followed a pattern that was to become familiar; first there was a very serious mauling of the NVA by superior firepower, then close contact that resulted in American dead and wounded, and finally withdrawal of the opposing forces. The First Cav did terrible damage, inflicting casualties at the rate of about five to one. The sad result was exactly opposite inferences by each side, revealed by interviews and archival research thirty years after the fact. The American staff in Saigon concluded that the enemy could not sustain such losses. Those in Hanoi were relieved that their forces had fought back, communicated and manoeuvred under heavy fire, and eventually did damage of their own. They were more than willing to accept the cost.

We faced an enemy unconstrained by democratic processes, who brooked no form of internal opposition; a state able and willing to place intransigent demands on its people. We were allied with a weak, temporizing, sometimes corrupt and often ineffective government that could neither impose its will nor secure its ends through popular enthusiasm. So we went on to a costly, bloody defeat; one that resulted in about 300,000 American and South Vietnamese dead and over a million Viet Cong and NVA dead. The total population of the North and

South was about 32 million people when this guide was written—by coincidence, about the same as that of the United States in 1860. The American Civil War resulted in over 600,000 deaths, more than the combined losses of all our other wars. There were twice as many Vietnamese killed. A generation of young men was consumed.

Most of this brutality lay ahead of us when I first read this book. Doubt and cynicism were creeping into the minds of American forces. At the peak of US forces in Vietnam every day saw about 1,500 men leave and 1,500 arrive from home, where open and sometimes violent dissent was growing. Staying alive and going home unharmed are always and everywhere the first desires of soldiers but especially so in Vietnam, where one started counting down the days immediately. Still, by and large, the American Army functioned and fought. There was no mass rebellion or desertion or widespread dissent. Merely the ordinary sort of resigned bitching that all soldiers everywhere employ as defence against the vast, impersonal beast that uses them for a time. And when I think of all those hundreds of thousands who went about their work, who counted their days and who would have laughed at the word 'duty' I am reminded that in their daily endeavours they embodied the guiding principles of this pocket guide. I think of them with affection and pride.

Bruns Grayson
Vietnam Veteran, US Army

HOW MUCH DO YOU KNOW ABOUT VIETNAM?

Farm family prepares tobacco for market.

NINE RULES
For Personnel of U.S. Military
Assistance Command, Vietnam

The Vietnamese have paid a heavy price in suffering for their long fight against the Communists. We military men are in Vietnam now because their government has asked us to help its soldiers and people in winning their struggle. The Viet Cong will attempt to turn the Vietnamese people against you. You can defeat them at every turn by the strength, understanding, and generosity you display with the people. Here are the nine simple rules:

"Remember we are special guests here; we make no demands and seek no special treatment.

"Join with the people! Understand their life, use phrases from their language, and honor their customs and laws.

"Treat women with politeness and respect.

"Make personal friends among the soldiers and common people.

"Always give the Vietnamese the right of way.

"Be alert to security and ready to react with your military skill.

"Don't attract attention by loud, rude, or unusual behavior.

"Avoid separating yourself from the people by a display of wealth or privilege.

"Above all else you are members of the U.S. military forces on a difficult mission, responsible for all your official and personal actions. Reflect honor upon yourself and the United States of America."

Fisherman mends his giant net.

OPPORTUNITY TO SERVE

If you are bound for Vietnam, it is for the deeply serious business of helping a brave nation repel Communist aggression. This is your official job and it is a vital one, not only for the preservation of freedom in this one country but for the survival of freedom everywhere.

Vietnam is a major testing ground for the Communists' theories of "wars of national liberation," and upon our success there depends peace in many other free countries of the world.

The growing American commitment in Vietnam makes it even more important for us to maintain the good relations that exist between Americans and the Vietnamese people. Wherever you go, remember that Vietnam is a land of dignity and reserve. Your good manners, thoughtfulness, and restrained behavior will be appreciated by the Vietnamese. You will benefit, as will the country you represent, in terms of the job you are there to do and in terms of friendship built on a solid foundation of mutual respect.

You can learn a great deal from the Vietnamese, who have been fighting for their country for many years, and you will find, as have many other Americans, that you will become greatly attached to them as individuals and as a people.

THE COUNTRY

When you reach South Vietnam you will be in a land with a civilization that predates the birth of Christ but which, since 1954, has been divided like Korea. North of the 17th parallel and Ben Hai River lies Communist North Vietnam and south is the free Republic of Vietnam.

The Republic of Vietnam is less than half the size of California and long and narrow like that State. It occupies the eastern and southern part of the Indochinese Peninsula in Southeast Asia, and borders the South China Sea and the Gulf of Siam. Near neighbors to the west are Laos, Cambodia, and Thailand. Beyond Communist Vietnam to the north stretches the vast territory of Red China.

The southern section of the rugged Annamite mountains forms a spine down to the Mekong Delta region around Saigon. In places, mountain spurs jut out to the sea, dividing the coastal plain into sections. Sand dunes 10 to 60 feet high are common along the long coastline.

The country is narrow up near Hué (pronounced whey)—so narrow that only a 30- to 50-mile strip lies between Laos and the South China Sea. Here the coastal rice fields very quickly give way to the uncultivated foothills of the mountains. In the past, lowland Vietnamese preferred to leave the mountains to tribespeople, wild animals, and evil spirits.

Southward from Hué toward the beach resort of Nha Trang, the country widens to make room for high plateaus, 1,000 to 3,000 feet above sea level. In the southern part of the country—around the Saigon-Cholon area—the many mouths of the Mekong River join a dense canal network to fan out across delta plains and nourish the fertile paddies of a bountiful "rice basket."

South Vietnam has a typically tropical climate of two seasons: hot and dry and hot and rainy.

In the southern delta region, the rains usually begin in late May and continue through September. April and early May are the hottest and most humid months of the year.

Along the central coast, the rainy season begins in October, causes periodic floods through November and December, and continues with drizzles from January to March. July and August are the months when heat and humidity reach their peak. In pleasant contrast, the highlands are usually cool at night regardless of the season.

Like other tropical countries, Vietnam has the usual variety of bugs, flies, mosquitos, and other insects. It's S.O.P. to sleep under a mosquito net.

Rice in the Deltas

This is an agricultural country with a soil-and-climate combination ideal for growing rice. With U.S. help, the South Vietnamese have greatly increased their rice production since 1954. You will find the paddies mainly in the Mekong River Delta and lowland areas of central Vietnam.

Its abundant rice crop, locally-grown vegetables, and fish from the richly-stocked seas at its door make the country largely self-sustaining in food.

A major export is rubber. Although the war ravaged the large rubber plantations and some of this acreage has not been reclaimed, rubber is still a very important product.

Lacquer from Vietnam has always been highly prized on the foreign market. It is used for mixing with other lacquers to improve their quality. The trees cultivated for extraction of lacquer are called *cay son*. Previously grown only in the north, the trees are being successfully experimented with in the southern highlands.

Relatively new as commercial products are palm oil from the plant formerly regarded by the Vietnamese as ornamental rather than useful, and peanuts which had been grown for home consumption but now are being exported in quantity both whole and as oil.

Tea, coffee, and quinine are grown in the high plateaus, which also produce cinnamon, timber, raw silk, vegetables, and vegetable dyes. Other Vietnamese products are corn, sugar cane, copra, tobacco, and mint oil.

The country has some cattle but more pigs and poultry. Water buffalo are used primarily as draft animals, especially in the rice paddies, and only occasionally for meat.

Muscle-powered sampans are typical of Mekong Delta.

No scene is more typical of rural Vietnam than a farmer and his water buffalo at work in a rice paddy. Water buffaloes are the indispensable work animals of the country.

Mineral resources are few: a coal-bearing region near the city of Da Nang (Tourane), south of Hué; a small gold mine, and scattered deposits of molybdenum and phosphate.

Industry is steadily expanding, though its scope is limited at present. New enterprises such as textile mills, cement plants, electronics, fish processing, and pharmaceuticals and plastics manufacture have been added to the traditional rice milling, lumber production, and manufacture of salt, beverages, soap, matches, and cigarettes.

Many free-world nations besides the United States are contributing economic assistance to help South Vietnam's agriculture and industry grow.

Picture the People

The population of the Republic of Vietnam is about 15.5 million, four-fifths of them farmers. (North Vietnam has an estimated 17 million people.) The majority of the people of South Vietnam are ethnic Vietnamese. There are almost 800,000 tribal people; close to one million Chinese (most of whom now hold Vietnamese citizenship); just under half a million ethnic Cambodians, and a few thousand each of French, Indians, and Pakistanis.

Compared with most Asian nations, South Vietnam is uncrowded. The population density varies from 19 per square mile throughout the six high plateau provinces to 43,100 people per square mile in Saigon, the capital. Saigon-Cholon is the largest city, with about two million people. Da Nang runs a distant second with about 130,000.

The Vietnamese are small and well-proportioned people, with dark, almond-shaped eyes and black hair. The slender, small-boned women move gracefully in their national dress of long trousers under a long-sleeved, tunic slit from hem to waist.

Most non-laboring Vietnamese men wear Western clothing on the street, but you will occasionally see traditional Chinese Mandarin robes. Workmen and peasants dress in loose black trousers and short black or white jackets. Their black jackets and trousers are similar to the black "pajama" uniforms worn by some of the Viet Cong and some Government paramilitary personnel.

Somewhat reserved and very polite, the Vietnamese are warm and friendly with people they like, and they are very cooperative and helpful. They have great respect for virtue and knowledge and honor older people. Many of their customs are conditioned by religious beliefs.

In the urban areas, French and English are second languages. Children study one or the other in school and increasingly English is their choice. But when you leave the cities, you may encounter even telephone operators who speak only Vietnamese.

Wisdom comes with age in Vietnam.

2,000 YEARS OF HISTORY

A Dragon and a Goddess

Vietnam has one of the world's oldest living civilizations. It dates back to hundreds of years before the birth of Christ, with roots in Asian religions and philosophies.

Legend has it that from the union of a dragon and a goddess came the hundred venerable ancestors of all Vietnamese. Belief in their common origin united the people and gave them a symbol around which to rally in the face of foreign invasion. Until 1955, the Vietnam coat-of-arms displayed a dragon carrying the country on its back. The coat-of-arms now features the bamboo plant.

The Viets originally occupied southern and southeastern China and the east coast of the Indochinese peninsula almost as far south as Hué, the old capital of Vietnam. In 111 B.C., their kingdom of Nam Viet was conquered by the Chinese, who controlled the country almost continuously for the next thousand years.

At times the Viet rebelled—usually unsuccessfully. A revolt led by the Trung sisters in 43 A.D. drove out the Chinese for a time. But the Chinese were vanquished only temporarily. In a few years they came back and the Trung sisters committed suicide by throwing themselves into the river.

The Viets made another courageous stand for survival as a free nation when, in 1284, they repulsed the Mongolian hordes of Kublai Khan. In the next century they pushed southward to conquer the once-great kingdom of Champa which occupied as much of what is now South Vietnam. They also met the Khmers (Cambodians) on the field of battle and forced them to retreat to their present boundaries.

Champa never recovered from its defeat by the Viets in Vijaya in 1471, and it disappeared from history during the 1700's. However, about 25,000 Chams who have never been assimilated into Vietnamese life still cluster in their own villages near Phan Rang, about midway down the coast. They follow a way of life scarcely distinguishable from that of unadvanced tribespeople in the area, and speak only their native Cham language.

Vietnam's Golden Age

Under the Le dynasty founded in the 15th century. Vietnam enjoyed a period of brilliant progress. Arts, crafts, agriculture, and commerce flourished. The code of laws developed during this time remained in effect until almost modern times.

The Le dynasty went through periods of strength and weakness. Two powerful families, the Trinh and the Nguyen, finally reduced the Le regime to puppet status and divided the country between themselves. The Trinh controlled the northern region, and the Nguyen controlled the central and southern regions of Vietnam.

In 1802 the last scion of the original Nguyen family—Gia Long—managed to gain the throne and unite all Vietnam under a single government administration and set of laws. In this enlightened era, there were schools in most villages, and foreign trade was encouraged and carried on through settlements of Dutch, Portuguese, French, and Japanese merchants in several towns.

The French Take Over

The French assumed control over the province of Cochin China in 1863. Before another decade has passed, the other two regions, Tonkin and Annam, also went under French rule. From that time until World War II, the country was part of French Indochina. The other two parts were Cambodia and Laos.

After the fall of France in 1940, the Japanese occupied French Indochina. This occupation continued until 1945 when Japan granted Vietnam independence under a puppet emperor, Bao Dai.

Meanwhile, by the time of the Japanese occupation, a group of expatriate, anti-French Vietnamese had formed in South China. One of these was Ho Chi Minh, a dedicated Communist, who entered Hanoi secretly in 1944. A year later, after Japan's surrender to the Allies, Ho's forces became the "Vietnam Liberation Army" and the shadow government of Emperor Bao Dai set up by Japan soon fell before the Communist leader's well-

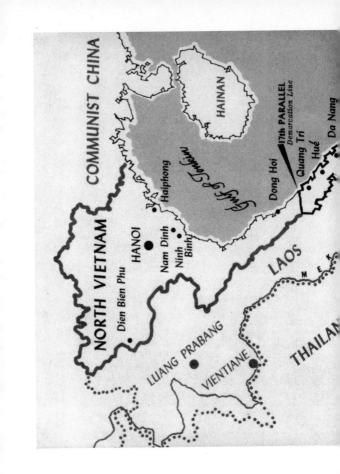

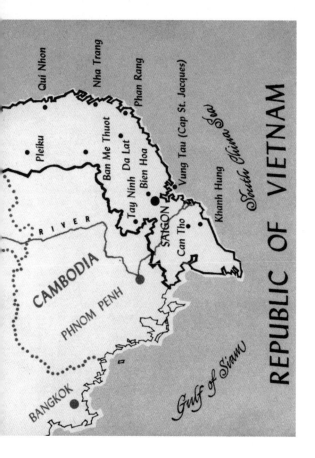

organized onslaught. The emperor abdicated, handing over his powers to Ho Chi Minh. At the same time, a "Provisional Executive Committee for South Vietnam," with seven Communists among its nine members, took control of Saigon.

Communists Show Their Hand

Like many other colonial people, the Vietnamese wanted national independence above all. That is why many followed Ho Chi Minh and the Communist-directed Viet Minh, which pretended to be a non-Communist league for the country's independence.

When the French tried to regain a foothold in Vietnam in 1946, Viet Minh forces attacked them on a wide front, supported by many people who had only one purpose—national independence. So began the costly 8-year Indochina war that ended with the division of Vietnam at a Geneva conference table in July 1954. The southern part of the country struck out as a free nation—the Republic of Vietnam—under the leadership of Ngo dinh Diem, with Saigon as its capital. The northern part of the country became the Communist-ruled Democratic Republic of Vietnam, with Hanoi as its capital.

THE REPUBLIC OF VIETNAM

A referendum in October 1955 offered the people of South Vietnam a choice between Emperor Bao Dai as chief of a state patterned on the old regime, and Ngo dinh Diem as chief of state of a republic. The vote was overwhelmingly in favor of the latter, and the Republic was proclaimed with Ngo dinh Diem as President.

The Republic of Vietnam has been recognized diplomatically by most of the free nations of the world. While not a member of the United Nations, it is represented on several specialized agencies of that body and regularly sends observers to U. N. meetings and to meetings of the Colombo Plan nations. It also participated officially in the Bandung Conference in 1955. Though not a member of the Southeast Asia Treaty Organization, South Vietnam is regarded as within the treaty area and its security is a direct concern of SEATO.

A constitutional assembly was elected in March 1956, and on July 7 a national constitution was adopted, making a good start toward showing what a determined nation can accomplish under dedicated leadership.

The war-ravaged country faced staggering problems— a ruined economy, an influx of 900,000 refugees from Communist North Vietnam, the rivalries of political factions, and the anti-Government activities of the Viet Cong, a subversive network the North Vietnamese had left in the South after the country was divided.

But through their own efforts, and with economic aid from the United States and other free-world countries, the South Vietnamese people began to prosper. By 1960, South Vietnam had made significant progress in agriculture, industry, health, education, and other fields. Rice and rubber production exceeded prewar production, the transportation system was largely rebuilt, and new industries were started. The number of primary school teachers tripled and school enrollment soared. Three thousand medical aid stations and maternity clinics were established throughout the country.

Increasing Viet Cong Activity

South Vietnam's progress stood in marked contrast to development in North Vietnam. The Communists in Hanoi had expected South Vietnam to collapse and fall into their hands like ripe fruit. Frustrated by its growing prosperity, the Communists in 1959 launched the Viet Cong guerrillas on an intensified campaign of guerrilla warfare and terrorist activities in the South. The following year, the Communist (Lao Dong) Party of North Vietnam organized the "National Front for the Liberation of South Vietnam," which it tried to disguise as a purely South Vietnamese nationalist organization.

Arms and men especially trained for sabotage and guerrilla warfare were infiltrated into the South. In the beginning, the cadres infiltrated were largely drawn from

A village elder samples water from a new well.

the 90,000 South Vietnamese who had gone North in 1954. Supported and directed by Hanoi, and actively encouraged with arms and aid from Communist China, the Viet Cong guerrillas attacked hamlets and villages; torturing, killing, or kidnapping the inhabitants who refused to cooperate with them. The Viet Cong murdered thousands of local officials, teachers, and health workers. Crowded trains and buses were bombed, roads destroyed, bridges and schools burned.

Help for a Sister Republic

After the Geneva accords of 1954 divided Vietnam, a U.S. Military Assistance Advisory Group (MAAG) became the only outside source of military aid for South Vietnam. Its mission was to improve the military effectiveness of the South Vietnamese Armed Forces.

But as the Viet Cong stepped up their terrorist and guerrilla campaign, it became clear that more help was needed, and President Diem appealed to the United States for increased assistance. Beginning in 1962, when the U.S. Military Assistance Command, Vietnam (MACV) was established, the United States has greatly increased both its military and economic aid and is prepared to do all that is necessary to help South Vietnam preserve its independence. We are not alone in giving this assistance. Thirty-six other free-world countries are also providing economic or military aid or both to South Vietnam, or have agreed to do so. And despite the increased tempo of the war, the economic aid programs in food, health, education, housing, and industry continue.

The Government

From 1956 to 1963 South Vietnam was governed under a constitution modeled in many respects on those of the United States and the Philippines, which provided for a strong executive, a unicameral National Assembly, and a judicial system. The Diem government, however, became increasingly personal and dictatorial. Opposition

Timber is trimmed in Vietnamese sawmill.

Schoolbooks capture the attention of young students.

was suppressed; there were charges of injustice and corruption against members of his family, particularly his brother, Ngo dinh Nhu; and President Diem lost in part the confidence and loyalty of the people. In 1963 serious political conflicts arose between the Government and the Buddhists, the largest single religious group in the country. Other non-Communist oppositionists to Diem made common cause with the Buddhists, and, on 1 November, 1963, the Diem government was overthrown by a military *coup d'etat.* Diem and his brother, Ngo dinh Nhu, who exercised great power in the regime, were killed.

Since then there has been considerable political instability in South Vietnam and a series of changes of government. In this connection, two things should be kept in mind: one, that the Vietnamese had little preparation for self-government and are struggling to develop unity and stability during a very dangerous internal security crisis caused by Communist aggression; and two, that not one of the groups competing for political power is in favor of accommodation with the Viet Cong.

Political activity has been confined chiefly to the cities and has had little impact on the great bulk of the population living in the countryside. These people— the villagers, the rice farmers, the rubber plantation workers—have had little feeling of identification with either the Viet Cong or the central Government. The Vietnamese farmer lives in a small world limited by the bamboo hedge around his village. His loyalties are to his family, his land, and his spiritual world. The Viet Cong have neutralized the people's support for the Government in some rural areas by a combination of terror and political action. One of the continuing programs of the central Government has been to provide better security and living conditions to convince the villagers that the Government the Communists seek to destroy is *their* Government.

Provinces and Districts

South Vietnam has 43 mainland provinces and five chartered cities—Saigon, Hué, Dalat, Da Nang, and

NEW RURAL LIFE HAMLETS

The new Rural Life Hamlet program, part of the Rural Reconstruction or Pacification program, is designed to provide physical safety, effective local government, and a better life for the rural population. A typical hamlet has rudimentary fortifications and warning systems. The inhabitants are trained and armed to protect themselves against Viet Cong attack until reinforcements arrive. As security improves, Government services in such fields as health, education, and agriculture are provided, in many cases with U. S. assistance. Local officials, who are trained and paid by the Government and administer the hamlet, are usually chosen in hamlet elections. The program is designed to provide the improved security and economic conditions that encourage loyalty to the central Government.

Vung Tau (Cap St. Jacques). Within the provinces are districts made up of a number of villages called *lang* in central Vietnam and *xa* in the south. The villages are made up of hamlets, (*ap*), which may be from a hundred yards to several miles apart. To at least eight of every 10 Vietnamese, "the Government" is the administrative group that runs his village.

Viet Cong hideout is captured by Vietnamese troops.

The Armed Forces

The Vietnamese have a long history of successful fighting against stronger and better equipped forces. They drove the Chinese from their land several times, repelled three Mongol invasions, and reduced the once powerful Champa Kingdom to nothing but a memory. One of their most famous generals, Tran Hung Dao, wrote a manual on military doctrine which has been a national classic on warfare for 600 years.

Under proper leadership, today's Vietnamese soldier is a tough brave fighting man who has stood up to 20 years of violence. He is worthy of your respect. Since 1960, some 30,000 members of the South Vietnamese armed forces have been killed and over 51,000 wounded in battle for their country. In proportion to population, these losses are 10 times as great as those suffered by Americans in the Korean war, and larger than our losses in World War II.

Vietnamese is decorated for defending his village.

Today the military power of the Republic of Vietnam is made up of three elements: the Regular Armed Forces (RVNAF), the Regional Force (formerly known as the Civil Guard), and the Popular Force (the former Self-Defense Corps), as well as elements of other militia or paramilitary organizations.

The Regular Armed Forces consist of the Army, Navy, Air Force, and Marine Corps, with the Army by far the largest. Of the other elements, often referred to as "paramilitary," the Regional Force most nearly approaches the Army in strength and capabilities. Its units, which do not exceed battalion strength, are usually stationed in the province in which organized.

The Popular Force is a regularly constituted militia composed largely of villagers who live and serve near their homes. Together with the Regional Force, they bear the brunt of the day-to-day fighting against the Viet Cong. In many ways these and other paramilitary groups could be compared to American minutemen during the Revolutionary War. They are being supplied with up-to-date weapons and field radios. The radios have filled a big communications gap. With them, help can be summoned fast or news of an impending attack flashed to the critical area.

The Army. The South Vietnamese Regular Army and paramilitary forces number more than 500,000 men. All physically fit young men of 20 and 21 are normally required to perform two years of military service. This requirement is altered to include additional age groups as the military situation dictates.

The Navy. Operating forces of the Navy consist of three major commands: the Sea Forces; the River Forces operating in the Mekong Delta Region; and the Marine Corps Group. A part of the shore establishment is the Junk Force organized as a paramilitary force and an inshore patrol force. It is manned in part by naval personnel, with Vietnamese fishermen providing the bulk of the force. Though small, the Navy is developing into a highly efficient organization.

The Air Force. About 12,000 officers and men—all volunteers—staff the Air Force. The force consists of transport, fighter, helicopter, and liaison squadrons, with necessary supporting units.

Your Legal Status

All official United States personnel are accorded diplomatic immunity by special concession of the Government of the Republic of Vietnam. Since military personnel are subject to U. S. military law, any local incident involving our military people is reported to the Commander, U. S. Military Assistance Command, Vietnam (COMUSMACV) for appropriate disciplinary action. This arrangement has worked out very well.

Determined-looking troops of Vietnamese Army.

Montagnard "Strike Force" was trained by Americans.

Vietnamese Government officials have expressed their satisfaction with the prompt and fair way such incidents as have occurred have been handled.

AT HOME WITH THE VIETNAMESE

You will find many areas of common interest with the Vietnamese: their regard for their families . . . their historic struggle for national independence . . . their wish to allow people individual freedom within the framework of laws made for the good of all.

But there are many differences between their culture and customs and our own and you must be prepared to deal with them in a way that will make you an acceptable friend of the Vietnamese.

A Vietnamese Navy Junk Force patrol.

Some of the differences are small things, like the way a Vietnamese seems to be waving goodbye when he is actually beckoning you to come toward him. You should not use typical American motions to beckon Vietnamese as they use such gestures only for animals. Also do not slap a man on the back unless you know him very well.

More important differences are attitudes toward older people, manual labor, display of emotion, and time. For instance, the average Vietnamese is less compulsive about time than the American, so you should not consider it a personal affront if people arrive late for an appointment or even if they don't arrive at all.

Moderation should be practiced in all things and the moral code of the people you are among strictly observed. Knowing that trouble breeds in situations where a person has one drink too many or forgets to

Armor protects Vietnamese Navy supply convoy.

show the utmost respect and courtesy toward women, you should make it a special point to avoid getting even close to the fringes of this sort of trouble. Never interfere in an argument among Vietnamese. A good general rule is to avoid all incidents that do not concern you directly.

Family Loyalty

The Vietnamese are justifiably proud of their culture and national identity, but their primary social outlook revolves around their family and village. These claim first allegiance. Members of a family, for instance, have an absolute obligation—to be violated only at the risk of serious dishonor—to care for their relatives and to prevent any of them from being in want. Even after a girl marries, her love and respect for her parents traditionally continue to overshadow her love and respect for her husband.

The traditional family unit includes living and dead members and members not yet born. On festival days and in family ceremonies the ancestors are revered, and at all times there is thought of the grandsons and great-grandsons yet to be born who will carry on the family name. A family without male heirs is assumed to have disappeared.

The importance of family is evident in the many terms used to denote family relationships. In addition to the usual ones like father, mother, brother, sister, the Vietnamese have terms to show relative age, the father's side of the family versus the mother's, and other niceties of relationship. In keeping with the lesser importance of younger people, there is only one term for a younger brother or sister. Either is *em*. But *anh* means elder brother and *chi*, elder sister.

Older people with their accumulation of a lifetime of experience are considered the wisest members of society and therefore are accorded the highest standing. If you are invited to a Vietnamese home for a meal, be sure to let the older people begin eating before you do. Be solicitous about helping them to things on the table.

Portrait of a Vietnamese farmer and his family.

Older Vietnamese, by the way, will usually not shake hands but will greet you by joining their hands in front of them and inclining their heads very slightly. Responding with the same gesture will show them that you know and appreciate this respectful custom.

Woman's Place Is at Home

Since the purpose of marriage is to continue the family line, the parents believe that the selection of a proper wife for their son is their personal responsibility, a duty they owe both to their ancestors and to their son and his future children. Usually with the help of a "go-between," they search for a girl who is skillful at housework and who will be a good mother to many children. Beauty is not as desirable as good character. In fact, beauty is sometimes considered a disadvantage because the Vietnamese believe that fate seldom is kind to beautiful women.

The traditional position of women is totally subordinate to men and their social life is limited. At the same time, wives often exercise a great deal of influence in the family, particularly in connection with financial affairs and, of course, in selecting marriage partners for their sons and daughters.

People of upper-class families, as well as people living in villages removed from big city and Western influences, continue to follow time-honored traditions and customs.

Young faces of Vietnam.

Among others, the customs have been considerably modified. Women are assuming a new and important position in the life of the nation, and young men and women are breaking away from tradition to choose their own marriage partners.

The Professional Man

The Vietnamese have always felt that a deep division exists between manual and "intellectual" labor. Traditionally Vietnamese who have achieved positions with the Government as a result of long and patient study, or who have become doctors, teachers, and so on, avoid using their hands for tasks they feel they have graduated beyond. It would be unusual, for example, to see such a person washing his car, helping his wife clear the table, or working in the garden.

Another thing, a Vietnamese might avoid looking a

superior in the eye when talking to him. This does not mean the man cannot be trusted. It means he is being polite by not "staring" at a person of greater standing.

At your first meeting with a Vietnamese he might ask: "How much money do you make?" This is a natural question in the sequence of "Are you married?" and "How many children do you have?" It simply expresses polite interest. If you feel uncomfortable about replying, you can avoid a direct answer by stating that you are paid in American dollars and don't know what the equivalent would be in Vietnamese currency. Your indirect reply lets the other person know you do not want to answer and have told him so politely. The matter is thus dropped without embarrassing anybody.

If you want to ask a favor, you should remember that hinting and indirection are preferable to making an outright request. Also avoid launching too quickly into a new topic or disagreeing too vehemently. Exercise moderation in your conversation. At a first meeting, it is often best to stay on safe topics like families or the weather.

Politeness and Restraint

Even among the most sophisticated Vietnamese, manners have not become lax or social customs unrestrained. Manners are conditioned by age-old religious teachings and are deeply ingrained in the life of the people.

Public display of emotion is almost always considered in bad taste. Raising the voice, shouting, or gesturing wildly are most impolite. Tied in with the view that marriage is primarily for continuance of the family line is a feeling that display of affection should be confined to the privacy of the home—and even there, not practiced before guests.

The Vietnamese regard men and women who walk arm-in-arm as vulgar. But you may occasionally see two boys or men walking down the street hand-in-hand. This is an ordinary mark of friendship common to many Asian and other countries.

If you follow the general practices of good manners and courtesy, and observe those that are particularly important to your Vietnamese hosts, you will be a welcome guest in Vietnam. This is vital to your mission there. You will fulfill your duty as a responsible representative of the United States best by remembering at all times that you are in a land where dignity, restraint, and politeness are highly regarded.

Town and Country

The architecture of homes in the cities and towns shows French and other Western influence, and decoration and furnishings also have a decidedly Western touch. But in the rural districts and mountain villages you will find thatched roofs, mud walls, pounded dirt floors, and little furniture. Some of the more pretentious rural houses have tile roofs, wooden walls, and floors of tile or flat brick squares set in mortar.

A feature of most homes is the family altar containing a tablet bearing the names of the family's ancestors going back at least to the great-grandfather. Veneration for the family's ancestors is perpetuated through the eldest son who is expected to succeed his father in caring for the altar. The altar may take up as much as one-sixth of the entire floor space of the house, excluding the kitchen. The kitchen is customarily built adjoining but separate from the living quarters.

Another interesting feature of a Vietnamese home is the plank bed. Often made of costly wood with inlaid mother-of-pearl, the bed may be as large as eight by

Army officer jokes with school children.

People of four mountain tribes live in this village.

five feet. Except for a mosquito net there is generally no bedding. The Vietnamese feel that in their hot climate it is more comfortable to sleep without bedding.

Village Life

The Vietnamese village, *lang* and *xa*, is an administrative unit rather like a county in the United States. It is made up of a number of scattered hamlets or *ap*, each set against a backdrop of bamboo thickets and groves of areca (betel nut) and coconut palms. Located at the village seat of government are a school, athletic or parade field, and a meeting hall. Some villages also have a dispensary and a maternity building containing a couple of beds and staffed by a trained midwife.

An "information" booth displays Government notices. Saigon newspapers may be kept here for public reference. The *dinh*, or village communal temple, houses a decree naming the village guardian spirit.

There is also a village market. On market day, which is once or twice a week, people file out of the hamlets to follow the narrow paths or rice paddy banks to the marketplace. They come to sell, to buy, or just to gossip. Some balance baskets of fresh fruits and vegetables on their heads.

A shopper can buy live chickens or duck eggs, conical hats to ward off the sun and plastic coats to keep away the rain, or Chinese herbs and Western aspirin, and even a brightly colored scarf in which to carry purchases.

A popular feature at the market is the man with a portable stove-and-bakery suspended from the ends of a bamboo pole balanced across his shoulders. From this ingenious double-duty device the merchant offers noodle soup on one side, papaya and red peppers on the other.

What's for Supper?

The average Vietnamese consumes less than two-thirds the calories the average American puts away every day. Starvation is extremely rare, but the basically vegetarian diet sometimes lacks proteins, vitamins, and minerals.

Most middle-class families have ample meals consisting of four types of foods: one salted, one fried or roasted, a vegetable soup, and rice. The soup (*canh*) is an important part of the meal and may contain bits of fish or meat along with the vegetables.

Rice is the staple food and its preparation is a grave responsibility for the women of the household. All girls are supposed to learn to cook as an essential part of their education. During the Moon Festival they prepare their best dishes so that the eligible bachelors may see how well they can cook—particularly *banh trung thu*—the special Moon Festival Cakes.

Fruits and Vegetables

The fruits and vegetables of Vietnam include many kinds familiar to you and others you may not know much about. Bananas, apples, pears, plums, oranges are among the familiar fruits; pomegranates and papayas, among the more exotic. Here you find the jujube—a sort of thorn tree with a fruit that flavors some of our candies—and the litchi, which is a fruit known in its dried form as "litchi nut." Among the vegetables are common ones like potatoes, turnips, carrots, onions, and beans; eggplant disguised under the name *aubergine*, and water bindweed, an herb that comes from the same family as our morning-glory flower.

Avoid eating raw vegetables or unpeeled fruit and drinking water that is not boiled or otherwise purified.

Vietnamese food delights both eye and palate.

The Fish Is Good

When the meal extends beyond vegetable and rice dishes, fish is generally served. More than 300 edible fish come from the sea and the inland waterways of Vietnam. Sole, mackerel, anchovy, tuna, squid, sardine, crab, and lobster are only a few. The tiny shrimp and oysters from the China Sea are particularly luscious, as are soups prepared from turtles caught on the beaches and in coastal waters.

The Vietnamese excel at preparing fish. Sometimes the fish is sautéed with onions, mushrooms, and vermicelli; or it may be slowly cooked with tomatoes, salted bamboo shoots, carrots, and leeks. Carp are often fried with celery. Eels make a banquet dish when sautéed in a sauce made of sugar, vinegar, rice flour, and sour-and-sweet soybean sauce. Another specialty is eel wrapped in aromatic leaves and grilled over charcoal, or boiled with green bananas, vegetables, saffron, and onions.

A fermented sauce made of fish and salt—*nuoc mam*—is almost as much a staple of diet as rice. It is served almost everywhere and with almost every meal. Many Westerners develop quite a taste for it.

Meat Dishes

Although Buddhism condemns the killing of living things, animals and fowl are killed for food. Pork is more commonly found on the average family's menu than beef.

It is roasted or sautéed with various vegetables and herbs. Lean pork baked in a crisp loaf with various seasonings, including cinnamon, is a tasty dish known as *cha-lua*.

A popular beef dish is made by cutting raw beef in thin slices and pouring boiling water over it, then promptly eating it with a dressing of soybean sauce and ginger. "Beef in seven dishes" is much appreciated by visitors as well as local people. One of these is a beef soup; in another, beef is cut into chunks or sliced, or else ground and formed in little balls or patties. Each has its own delicious sauce.

Hens are prepared to a gourmet's taste by stuffing with aromatic vegetables, seasoned with salt, pepper, garlic, and basted with coconut milk while roasting; or, after boning, by filling with meat, chestnuts, mushrooms, and onions and basting with honey while baking.

Tea at All Times

Tea is the principal Vietnamese beverage in the morning, afternoon, and evening—for any occasion or no occasion at all. At mealtime it is usually served after the meal rather than with it. Chinese tea is much appreciated, particularly when flavored with lotus or jasmine, but it is too expensive for most people. They use the local teas: dried (*che-kho*), roasted (*che-man*), or dried flower-buds, (*che-nu*). Tea, incidentally, is an acceptable gift under almost any circumstance.

When coffee is served, it is generally offered with milk as *café au lait* in the morning, or black as *café noir* for an after-dinner demi-tasse.

In towns and cities you can generally get cognac, whiskey, French wines, and champagne.

Alcoholic beverages produced locally are principally beer and *ruou nep*, made from fermented glutinous rice.

Festivals and Lunar Calendar

Outside of the larger cities and the relatively few Christian areas, the routine of work goes on day after day without a pause on the seventh. From dawn to dark the father tills the fields or casts his nets for fish; the women and all but the very young children help in the paddies or tend to household duties. Only when there is a national holiday or religious festival does the daily routine of "work, eat, sleep" come to a temporary halt.

The following poem expresses the ritual of Vietnamese life and festivals:

> January, celebrate the New Year at home;
> February, gambling; March, local festivals;
> April, cook bean pudding;
> Celebrate the feast of *Doan Ngo* at the return of May;
> June, buy *longans* and sell wild cherries;
> At the mid-July full moon, pardon the wandering
>   spirits;

44

August, celebrate the lantern festival;

At the return of September, sell persimmons with the others;

October, buy paddy (unhulled rice) and sell kapok;

November and December, work is finished.

All of the festivals mentioned in the poem are based on the lunar calendar. This causes the dates to vary from year to year by our calendar, like our Easter.

The Vietnamese lunar calendar, like the Chinese, begins with the year 2637 B.C. It has 12 months of 29 or 30 days each, totaling 355 days. Every third year or so an extra month is slipped in between the third and fourth months to reconcile the lunar calendar with the solar calendar. An advantage of the lunar calendar (at least to moon-minded people) is that you can count on a full moon on the 15th day of each month.

Instead of centuries of 100 years each, the Vietnamese calendar is divided into 60-year periods. Each year in one of these periods is designated by one of five elements and one of 12 animals: Wood, fire, earth, metal, water; and rat, buffalo, tiger, cat, dragon, snake, horse, goat, monkey, chicken, dog, and pig. The year 1966—which is the Vietnamese year 4603—is designated by the combination of wood and horse, but you will commonly hear it referred to as "Year of the Horse," just as 1965 was called the "Year of the Snake."

Tet Nguyen Dan (New Year) is observed quietly by some.

Annual Festivals

The chief Vietnamese festivals by the lunar calendar are:

- The New Year, *Tet Nguyen Dan*, 1st through 7th day of 1st month;

- The Summer Solstice, *Doan Ngo*, 5th day of the 5th month;

Tet Nguyen Dan is celebrated boisterously by others.

- Wandering Souls, *Trung Nguyen*, 15th day of the 7th month; also celebrated on the 15th day of the 1st and 10th months;

- Mid-Autumn, *Trung Thu*, 15th day of the 8th month;

- *Tran Hung Dao*, 20th day of the 8th month; and

- *Le Loi*, 22nd of the 8th month.

The Tet Nguyen Dan, or New Year, often called "Tet," is the big event of the year. It marks the beginning of spring, and by the solar calendar usually falls toward the end of January or in early February. All work usually stops for the first three days, and most shops are closed.

Vietnamese tradition attaches great significance to the first visitor of the New Year. He is thought to influence the happiness or well-being of the family during the entire year. If a rich man or one with a lot of children or one of high social position is the first to cross the threshold, the family's fortunes will be correspondingly

Religion is important to the Vietnamese.

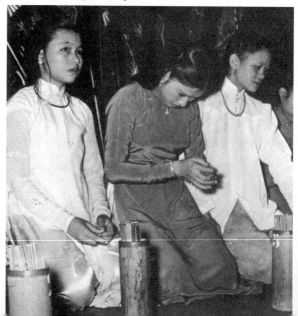

affected. A happy man with a good name like *Phuoc* (happiness) is preferable to a sad man or one named *Cho* (dog). In fact, some families go out of their way to invite a propitious first guest, and to discourage all others from entering before him.

Eating the New Year's cake, *banh chung*, is another means of insuring prosperity. The cake consists of a combination of sticky rice, pork, and soybeans wrapped in green bamboo or rush leaves, and then boiled.

At the time of the New Year, new clothes are in order and old debts are settled.

The festival begins with veneration at the family shrine and public worship with people carrying lighted candles and incense. There are presents for the children, feasts, and gay, noisy public celebrations. Firecrackers are forbidden during wartime, but there is always the sound of gongs and cymbals and the traditional unicorn dance. The unicorn brings luck, especially to those who hang money from their windows for the unicorn to eat!

Religion Can Be Plural

Instead of saying one religion is right and all others wrong, the Vietnamese are more apt to take the position that one is right and another is not wrong either. For instance, a man who makes offerings in a Buddhist temple probably also pays reverence to the ancestral altar in his own home in keeping with the teachings of Confucius.

You may even find Christ, Confucius, Mohammed, and Buddha all honored in the same temple.

Consequently, it is not too meaningful to say that a certain percentage of the Vietnamese are Buddhists and another percent something else. The percentages may be made up of individuals who are both Buddhists and something else.

Religion has been a significant factor in the Vietnam way of life throughout history. The present culture and customs of these proud and sensitive people are strongly conditioned by their religious beliefs. For example, feeling that the universe and man's place in it are essentially preordained and unchanging, they place high value on stoicism, patience, courage, and resiliency in the face of adversity.

To get along in Vietnam you must have some understanding of these traditional beliefs. If, for instance, you did not know that the parts of the human body are believed to possess varying degrees of worthiness—starting with the head—you would not see why patting a person on the head might be considered a gross insult. Or why it would be insulting for you to sit with your legs crossed and pointed toward some individual. Either of these actions could cause you to be regarded in a poor light by Vietnamese who follow the traditional ways.

Religion is an important element in the political views most Vietnamese have, and religious leaders in recent years have played an increasingly active role in Vietnamese politics.

Confucianism. Confucianism, a philosophy brought to Vietnam centuries ago by the Chinese, not only has been a major religion for centuries, but also has contributed immensely to the development of the cultural, moral, and political life of the country. It establishes a code of relations between people, the most important being the relation between sovereign and subject, father and son, wife and husband, younger to older people, friend to friend. Teaching that disorders in a group spring from improper conduct on the part of its individual members, achievement of harmony is held to be the first duty of every Confucianist.

When he dies, the Confucianist is revered as an ancestor who is joined forever to nature. His children honor and preserve his memory in solemn ancestor rites. At the family shrine containing the ancestral tablets, the head of each family respectfully reports to his ancestors all important family events and seeks their advice.

Buddhism. Confucianism goes hand in hand in many Vietnamese homes with Buddhism, a religion first taught in India some 26 centuries ago by Prince Gautama, also known as the Gautama Buddha. Buddhism was introduced into Vietnam about the 2nd century B.C. by Chinese and Hindu monks. In Buddhism the individual finds a larger

Buddhist rites are ages old.

meaning to life by establishing identity with eternity—
past, present, future—through cycles of reincarnation. In
the hope of eventual *nirvana*, that is, oneness with the
universe, he finds consolation in times of bereavement and
special joy in times of weddings and births.

The *Greater Vehicle* (*Mahayana*) form has more
followers than the *Lesser Vehicle* (*Therevada*) in Vietnam,
as also in China, Korea, and Japan. This branch regards

the Gautama Buddha as only one of many Buddhas (Enlightened Ones) who are manifestations of the fundamental divine power of the universe. They believe that, theoretically, any person may become a Buddha, though those who attain Buddhahood are rare. Saints who earnestly strive for such perfection are known as *bodhisattvas*. Both Buddhas and bodhisattvas are recognized and venerated in Mahayana temples.

Lesser Vehicle believers follow the teachings of Gautama and regard him as the only Buddha. In the southern delta provinces of Vietnam, particularly in Vinh Binh, Ba Xuyen, and An Giang where there are large groups of ethnic Cambodians, you will often see the saffron-robed monks of the Lesser Vehicle. This branch is also found in Ceylon, Burma, Thailand, Cambodia, and Laos—in other words, in those countries that had a dominant Indian rather than a dominant Chinese historical influence.

Pagodas, originally established as Buddhist monasteries and monastic study centers, now often serve also as social welfare institutions, and may include schools, orphanages, medical dispensaries, public libraries, and youth clubs.

Although the number of devout, practicing Buddhists in South Vietnam is relatively small, the great majority of the people have some sense of identification with Buddhism. In recent years, leading Buddhist priests (*bonzes*) have become increasingly active in political

53

Procession before Saigon's Catholic Cathedral

affairs and influential in the rise and fall of South Vietnamese governments.

Christianity. Christianity reached Vietnam in the 16th and 17th centuries, mainly through the efforts of Roman Catholic Spanish and Portuguese missionaries. As a result of persistent missionary efforts—frequently in the face of persecution by emperors who feared Western political and economic control—approximately 10 percent of the population of the Republic of Vietnam are Catholics. This is the highest proportion of Catholics in any Asian country except the Philippines.

American Protestant missions have been in Vietnam since World War I. At first their activities were mainly limited to the mountain tribes of the high plateaus. With the gradual rise of American assistance and influence, there has been an increase in Protestant activity in the lowlands. Baptist, Mennonite, Christian and Missionary Alliance, and Seventh Day Adventist missions now exist in several cities, and some Vietnamese Protestant students are being sent to the United States for advanced help in theological training.

New Religions. In addition to the religions and philosophies brought to Vietnam from other countries, new ones were developed there. Chief among these were the Cao Dai and the Hoa Hao.

Cao Dai is a blend of the three great oriental philosophies—Confucianism, Taoism, and Buddhism—set in an organizational structure based on that of the Roman Catholic Church. The head of the church, the "Superior," fills a position similar to that of the Pope.

At one time Cao Dai claimed a following of 3 million. Now the religion is less widely practiced, but you may still see Cao Dai temples throughout Vietnam. The

This elaborate Cao Dai temple is near Tay Ninh.

cathedral near the city of Tay Ninh, about 55 miles northwest of Saigon, is the largest and best known. Built between 1933 and 1941, it is located not far from the revered Nui Ba Den, Mountain of the Black Virgin. The mountain is a holy place of the Buddhist faith, one to which pilgrimages have long been made.

Hoa Hao is an offshoot of Buddhism that came into being in An Giang province in southwest Vietnam in

1919. Its founder was a young man named Huynh Phu So, and he gave the new religion the name of his village of birth. He became famous as a teacher and miracle healer, preaching that temples, rituals, and priests were not necessary to the worship of God. This greatly appealed to the poor people and peasants. Some 20 years after its founding, Hoa Hao had a million and a half or more followers, though Viet Minh Communists murdered the founder in 1947 and no leader of comparable stature appeared to take his place.

Education and Culture

Regardless of the changes the Vietnamese have passed through—from the rule of their own emperors to rule by French governors to the present republican government—one factor that has remained constant is their inherent reverence for learning.

Under the Confucian social system, the scholar stood at the head of the occupational hierarchy. The scholar received the highest economic, social, and political rewards. The nation was governed at all levels of administration by officials who were chosen on the basis of education alone. The aristocracy of learning was the only aristocracy of any continuing importance in old Vietnam. Education, especially in Chinese philosophy and history, was not only prized for its own sake but was the main road to wealth, power, and social standing.

With the coming of the French, the formal educational system changed considerably. Beginning in the 19th century, the French encouraged the Vietnamese to write their own language in the Latin alphabet.

Public Schools. The present school system retains substantially the form of the French school system. In addition, the Government is attempting to raise the literacy rate among older people through evening classes.

Primary schools have a 5-year curriculum and the first three grades are compulsory for all children.

Secondary schools have two divisions with a 4-year course in the first, and a 3-year course in the second. The 4-year course is divided into classical and modern sections. In addition to basic subjects, those choosing the classical course take Vietnamese literature and Chinese characters, while pupils in the modern section take history, French, and English.

The 3-year course continues the general pattern of the first, but gives students the option of continuing their language studies or of substituting programs of natural science or of mathematics and philosophy.

The goal of secondary education is to pass the stiff baccalaureate examinations required for admission to the 5-year university program or to the advanced technical schools.

Private Schools, Universities. In addition to public schools at the primary and secondary levels, there are both religious and secular private schools. These schools follow the public-school curriculum and are regulated and subsidized by the Department of Education.

In addition, there are a number of normal schools which train schoolteachers, an industrial technical school, other specialized governmental technical schools, and a school of applied arts, where the traditional fine arts of Vietnam are taught. These include gold-smithing, lacquer work, cabinetwork, and pottery making.

The National University of Vietnam in Saigon is the most important institution of higher education. There also are universities at Dalat and Hué, and several technical schools of university rank, including the National Institute of Administration in Saigon.

Higher education in foreign countries is greatly sought after by advanced students. The Vietnamese Government grants passports for study abroad to students wanting to study courses not offered in Vietnam, and at least 1,000 to 1,500 Vietnamese students will be abroad in any year.

Youth Movements such as Boy Scouts, sports clubs, and sectarian organizations of the Christian and Buddhist youth have had a strong revival. A Cabinet-level agency under the Government is responsible for encouraging and supporting youth activities.

Since 1963 high school and university students have become increasingly interested and active in political and social matters. Their community services have included massive participation in relief operations after the disastrous floods of 1964 as well as many smaller assistance projects. Efforts are now underway to get Vietnamese youth even more involved in the vital task of preserving national independence.

A Rich Culture

The admiration and honor accorded scholars by the Vietnamese extends to writers, especially poets, and the literature of the nation is rich and sensitive.

The painting, sculpture, and other arts of Vietnam are vigorous and imaginative, with lively motifs of dragons, tigers, elephants, unicorns, and horses. The fabled phoenix and other birds, the tortoise, bamboo, and exotic flowers also figure in the designs. Artists create most intricate designs, though the tools and materials they use are often very simple.

The country is known for its woodcarving, mother-of-pearl inlay, lacquer and metal work. You can see the artistry of skilled metal-smiths in the beautiful bronze decorations in pagodas, temples, palaces, and public buildings, and in statues, perfume and incense burners, candlesticks and so on. Tin, pewter, and copper are also used to create art objects of long-enduring beauty and usefulness.

Embroidery and mat weaving are crafts widely practiced. A grateful people even created a temple at Hai Thien in honor of Pham Don Le, the Mandarin who established mat weaving in Vietnam. Traditional mat decorations include the symbol for longevity, and often the design includes bats or butterflies in the corners of the rug to signify happiness.

Theater and Music

Should you get a chance to go to the theater you may enjoy the *cai luong*, or modern form, more than the *hat boi*, or classical style. The classical theater uses colorful costuming and scenery, and the plays are very tragic and

Dragons guard war memorial entrance in Saigon.

dramatic. The modern theater, which came into being around 1920 cuts to a minimum scenery, costumes, and stage effects, and the stories are less heroic and more realistic.

The music of Vietnam will be most strange to your ears until you get used to it. A scale of five notes and two semi-notes is used and the classical instruments are various stringed instruments, drums, and gongs. In the classical theater the acting is stressed with laments from the strings and vigorous noise from drums and gongs.

MOUNTAIN TRIBESPEOPLE

Tribal people outnumber the ethnic Vietnamese at places on or near Vietnam's high plateau. They formerly lived along the coast of north and central Vietnam. About the time of Christ's birth, powerful nations like Funan and Champa forced them out of their coastal villages into the mountains. They are estimated to number almost 800,000.

You may hear these people called *"montagnard"* or "moi". The first is a French word meaning "mountaineer." The second is a Vietnamese term meaning "savage" or "barbarian," which is understandably resented by them. Two terms much more acceptable to them are *dong bao thuong*, meaning "highland compatriot," and *nugoi*

Rhade girls carry water home in gourds.

thuong du, meaning "highland people." A good English word is "tribespeople," since it describes their way of life without uncomplimentary meanings.

Appearance and Language

Tribespeople of different villages quite often are unable to understand each other's language and also have marked physical differences. Depending on the tribe, their skin color varies from extremely dark to shghtly bronzed white. Some are tall and well-built, others short and slight. Their hair may be frizzy or straight; and their clothing may cover more of their bodies than your uniform does of yours, or consist of nothing more than a few beads and a g-string.

The more than a score of different tribes can be grouped in two broad classifications based on language. Those in the larger group speak languages of the Mon-khmer linguistic family related to present-day Cambodian. Some of these are *Baru*, *Katu*, *Cua*, *Sedang*, *Hrey*, *Bahnar*, *Koho*, *Steing*, *Maong*, and *Ma*.

Those in the smaller group speak languages of the Malayo-Poly-nesian linguistic family that are related to Cham. The principal tribes speaking languages of this family are *Rhade*, *Jarai*, and *Raglai*.

But even within a language group, people of one village sometimes cannot understand those of another. If 10 to 20 miles of matted jungle trail separate the villages, there is not much communication between them and language differences develop.

Languages of both these two linguistic families Mon-Khmer and Malayo-Polynesian, differ greatly from Vietnamese in at least one major respect—they have no differing tones, while Vietnamese does. Since tones are usually difficult for Americans, tribal languages should be easier for you to learn than Vietnamese.

Also, none of these people ever had a written language of their own until French and American missionaries began devising them, mostly in this century. Comparatively few tribespeople know how to read, so if you want to study their language you do so by ear not by book.

The Spirit World

Despite many differences, some basic characteristics are shared by almost all of the tribespeople.

First of all, superstitions and fear play a heavy role in their lives. Although Christian missionary efforts have made some changes, the great majority of tribespeople are animists or spirit believers. Followers of this ancient Southeast Asian religion believe that practically everything has its own spirit—a rock, for example, or a tree. Most of the spirits are unfriendly, and tribespeople take elaborate precautions to avoid antagonizing them.

Casting one's shadow on a particular rock, for

instance, may offend the spirit of the rock and cause it to take vengeance on the careless human. On the advice of a witch doctor, a tribesman will sacrifice a pig or even a water buffalo to appease an angry spirit. On a single day one Koho village near the town of Di Linh in Lam Dong Province sacrificed 42 water buffalo to make peace with the spirits.

Wealth in Jars

Every tribal home has its gongs and jars, chiefly used for ceremonies and festivals. The gongs, as you guessed, are for making noise; the jars hold various household supplies and are used to brew an alcoholic holiday drink for community celebrations, like the arrival of strangers, a buffalo sacrifice, or any other likely reason.

The drink is brewed by putting the branch of a special tree or bush in the jar, then alcohol, and then filling the jar to the brim with water from a nearby creek. You then sit with the male villagers in a circle around the jar. Each person, in turn, beginning with the village chief, takes a generous swig from the jar through a bent bamboo straw that is often over six feet long (everybody using the same straw, of course). As each person drinks, a designated villager uses a dipper to transfer water from a nearby pot to the jar, being careful to refill the jar to the brim each time. Thus, the drinking may continue indefinitely, yet the jar always remains full.

After the first round, you can stop drinking without giving offense. The drink is not strong, and should affect you only if taken in great quantity. These drinking celebrations often accompany animal sacrifices.

Tribal Hospitality

Besides almost universal superstition and fear of unfriendly spirits, another characteristic most tribes have in common is open-handed hospitality to strangers. If you arrive in a Ma village, for instance, you will probably be offered sleeping space in the chief's house as well as food.

Ma houses, like those of practically all tribespeople except the *Jeh* and *Katu*, are single-story dwellings raised several feet from ground level by pillars or stilts. Raising the house provides a shaded refuge from the sun underneath the house and discourages night entrance by wild animals such as tigers. The roofs are low and have center peaks.

The Ma build their houses as long as the hillside will permit. Some, though only about six feet wide, are over 120 feet long and accommodate several families. Each family has a separate entrance—consisting of stairway, platform, and doorway—along one of the two long sides of the structure. Each family also has its own hearth. There are no partitions and you can see from one end to the other.

If you plan to visit tribespeople in any region you will receive an even warmer reception if you bring gifts of medicine or salt. Local aspirin is quite inexpensive and salt is extremely cheap, but tribespeople prize both items highly because they have almost no money.

Don't be too handy with your camera, especially if it is the kind that produces a print on the spot. Before trying to take any pictures, explain about the camera and if there is some reservation on the part of the subject—don't shoot! Many Vietnamese, like many of us, would be flattered to have their pictures taken and given to them right away, but tribesmen, because of their spirit beliefs, may become quite upset. To them you have captured their spirit and imprisoned it in the picture. One well-meaning missionary who handed a tribesman such a print was arrested by the whole village and only set free after he had agreed to pay for a sacrificial pig in atonement.

GETTING AROUND

For a small country, South Vietnam has a great variety of attractions. Saigon offers fascinating shops and markets; Hué, great sightseeing possibilities. There are many beautiful white sand beaches along the country's thousand miles of coastline. Some are always accessible. Access to others depends on the military situation.

National Assembly meets in a white building.

Saigon—Cholon

Saigon is the capital and largest city of Vietnam. With its predominantly Chinese city of Cholon (meaning "big market"), it lies about 50 miles inland from the South China Sea on the navigable Saigon River. It is a busy commercial port and has all of the hustle and bustle of a port city plus a lot of color and confusion uniquely its own.

The water traffic on the river includes ocean-going vessels as well as assorted small boats, junks, and fishing craft. On the city streets the traffic is even more varied. There are motor scooters, pedicabs, bicycles, automobiles—and pedestrians in Asian or Western dress or something in between. From the sidelines, the relaxed patrons of the many sidewalk cafes sip their tea or beer and watch the world go by.

Saigon has museums where you can see relics of past civilizations, including the Cham. Or you may wander along Duong Tu Do (Freedom Street), the fashionable shopping center, theater, and cafe area. At one end of Tu Do stands the post office and Catholic Cathedral. Not far from the Cathedral is the executive mansion, named Independence Palace.

A place you cannot miss is the Saigon Central Market. Here, under a single roof of a clean-lined modern building, you can buy an amazing variety of things; fish, brassware, vegetables, a length of cloth, and a hundred other necessities or luxury items.

The excellent restaurants of both Saigon and Cholon will tempt you. Try the specialties of the house but remember to be wary of raw vegetables or unpeeled fruits and *never* eat raw pork. Excellent French cooking vies with interesting Vietnamese dishes and in Cholon you will find Chinese delicacies such as sharkfin soup and Szechwan duck.

Hué

Hué, the former royal capital, is located at the other end of the country near the North Vietnam border.

Be sure to examine the remains of the citadel built on the model of Peking. A moat surrounds *Thanh Noi*, the Interior City, and another encircles *Dai Noi*, the Great Interior, which once housed the emperor and his retinue.

The former imperial Palace in Hué

Nearly 100 buildings were clustered in this section until the Communists blew them up in 1945 in an attempt to sever Vietnam from its past.

The Government has restored a few of the buildings. You can see the Emperor's Audience Hall with its gilt throne and red, dragon-decorated pillars. A children's classical ballet troop, supported by the Government as a carryover from the royal ballet, still performs on festival days along the steps in front of the Audience Hall.

In front of the royal citadel, sampans drift on the Perfume River as it makes its slow way to the nearby sea. On the night of a full moon, you can rent one of these sampans with its interior of costly wood and inlaid mother-of-pearl, hire a singer and four musicians, and float along the river to the music of the singers' wails mingled with the twang of the instruments' strings. Small market-boats ply the river and will offer you bottled drinks, exotic fruits, and lotus buds freshly plucked from the imperial moat.

Hué's oldest building is a Buddhist temple, erected on the banks of the Perfume River by Nguyen Hoang in 1601 to commemorate a vision he had in which an old woman predicted that he would be the founder of a flourishing dynasty. He was 76 at the time, but the prediction came true. Later, in 1844, a seven-story tower, the Phuoc Duyen, was built in front of the temple. This is Hué's most famous landmark.

The rolling hills south of the city contain thousands of tombs, including six royal ones. The latter are large park-like enclosures behind massive gates. Some have ponds, delicate trees, and even little temples. Many of the emperors began constructing their tombs long before death, and at least two of them, Minh Mang and Tu Duc, used them as a sort of summer palace for relaxing, contemplating nature, and writing poetry. Best preserved is the gracious enclosure built by Minh Mang, with its many frangipani and flowering almond trees, and curving, lotus-clogged ponds.

Da Nang

Da Nang is a coastal town 60 miles south of Hué, separated from Hué by a finger of the mountains that juts into the sea. The road between the two cities, which is not always secure for travel, crosses a narrow pass where traffic flows only one way at a time. If you forget to time your trip with control of this traffic, you may find yourself caught in an hour or more delay.

Nha Trang

On down the coast lies Nha Trang, about 198 statute miles northeast of Saigon. Here you can enjoy all sorts of water sports—swimming, skin-diving, water-skiing— or make a trip to one of the offshore islands in the bay. You also can visit the aquarium and the Institute of Oceanography at Cau-Da, or see the old Cham tower, Thao Ba, now used as a Buddhist Temple.

Dalat

Dalat is a small, exquisite mountain resort surrounded by pine-covered hills in central Vietnam. Situated at a 5,000-foot elevation, it has cool nights throughout the year. But in the rainy season it's wet! By August the rains are falling almost continuously. Books, leather goods, food, and clothing mildew unless stored in a "hot closet" which has a light bulb burning constantly.

The town is the home of the National Military Academy, the Armed Forces Command and General Staff College, and the Geographic Institute of Vietnam.

It is the center of a small sightseeing area of mountains, lakes, waterfalls, and has a lovely artificial lake of its own. Craftwork of the mountain tribespeople is on sale in the local markets. You can buy their baskets, jewelry, pipes, handwoven materials, and native musical instruments; even fresh orchids. As a matter of fact, Dalat is an orchid center. Some 1,500 varieties are grown in the spacious greenhouses of the town's many flower fanciers.

Vung Tau (Cap St. Jacques)

This interesting little town on the South China Sea is now officially called Vung Tau but is also still known by its former French name of Cap St. Jacques. It is about 50 miles from Saigon and its beaches are excellent.

SERVICE WITH SATISFACTION

You who help the Vietnamese maintain their freedom will have many fine things to remember about the people and the country. You will have the satisfaction of sharing the experience of a staunch and dedicated nation in a most critical period of its history. In a broader sense, you will be helping to block the spread of communism through Southeast Asia.

Your exemplary conduct—making a good compromise between the more informal ways of our country and the traditional ones of Vietnam—will do a lot toward bridging the gap between East and West. This is essential, as the success of your minion requires that you build up a good relationship with the South Vietnamese people. This can be done only through day-by-day association with them on terms of mutual confidence and respect, both while doing your military job and in your off-duty hours. You'll find opportunity for recreation, but the Vietnamese will also appreciate a helping hand on local civic projects, such as improving sanitary, medical, or transportation facilities, and building a playground or school.

You will find that life in South Vietnam can be frustrating, tense, and at times full of danger. But you will also find that it brings great rewards.

APPENDIX

Time

Vietnam is 13 hours ahead of our Eastern Standard time. For example, when it is 12 noon, EST, in New York or Washington, D. C., it is one a.m. the next day in Vietnam. Also, when it is midnight in New York or Washington, it is one p.m. the same day in Vietnam.

Money

South Vietnam's unit of money is the *piaster* or *dong*. Notes are issued in denominations of 1, 2, 5, 10, 20, 50, 100, 200, and 500 piasters or dong.

U.S. military and civilian personnel serving in Vietnam are paid in Military Payment Certificates (MPC's), issued in the same denominations as U.S. currency. The MPC's, also called "scrip", can only be used in official facilities, such as exchanges, commissaries, clubs, and messes.

Piasters may be purchased at official exchange points at the rate of 118 piasters for 1 dollar.

Weights and Measures

The international metric system of weights and measures is used throughout Vietnam. Gasoline and other liquids are sold by the liter (1.0567 liquid quarts); cloth by the meter (39 inches); food and other weighed items by the kilogram (2.2 pounds). Distance is measured by the kilometer (0.62 mile); speed in kilometers per hour (25 k.p.h. equals 15 m.p.h.).

Distance and Speed Conversion

Kilometers	1	2	3	4	5	10	25	50	100	500
Miles	6	1.2	1.8	2.5	3	6	15	31	62	311

Gasoline Conversion

Liters	3.8	7.6	11.4	15.1	18.9	37.9	56.8	76.8
Gallons	1	2	3	4	5	10	15	20

SUGGESTED READING

Armed Forces and Education, *Aggression From the North: The Record of North Vietnam's Campaign to Conquer South Vietnam* (DoD GEN–14).
  Evidence at Vung Ro Bay (DoD GEN–16).
  The Struggle in South Vietnam: 'Liberation' or Conquest? (DoD GEN–19).
  Vietnam: Four Steps to Peace (DoD GEN–18).
  Vietnam: The Struggle for Freedom (DoD GEN–8).
  Why Vietnam? (Unnumbered).
Browne, Malcolm W., *The New Face of War*. Bobbs-Merrill Co., Inc., Indianapolis, 1965.

Buttinger, Joseph, *The Smaller Dragon: A Political History of Vietnam.* Frederick A. Praeger, New York, 1958.

Carver, Jr., George A., *The Real Revolution in South Vietnam.* Foreign Affairs, April, 1965.

Halberstam, David, *The Making of a Quagmire.* Random House, Inc., New York, 1965.

Huong Van Chi, *From Colonialism to Communism: A Case History of North Vietnam.* Frederick A. Praeger, New York, 1964.

Fishel, Wesley R., ed., *Problems of Freedom: South Vietnam Since Independence.* Free Press of Glencoe, New York, 1961.

Lansdale, Edward G., *Vietnam: Do We Understand Revolution?* Foreign Affairs, October, 1964.

Tregaskis, Richard, *Vietnam Diary.* Holt, Rinehart & Winston, Inc., New York, 1963.

VIETNAMESE LANGUAGE GUIDE

Some 27,000,000 people speak Vietnamese as their first language. The great majority of them live in Viet-Nam. Others are in Cambodia, Laos, Thailand, France, and New Caledonia.

Vietnamese was first written in Chinese characters, then in the late thirteenth century, in a modified form called *chú nôm*. In the early 1600's, Portuguese and Italian Jesuit missionaries devised a system of writing Vietnamese with the Latin alphabet. Chinese characters and *chú nôm* continued in use through the early part of this century but were officially replaced in 1920 by Latin script. This is called *quốc ngũ* and consists of 12 vowel and 27 consonant forms.

The simple vowels are: a, e, i, o, u, and y. Modifications of these vowels add six more to the alphabet. The modifications are indicated by diacritical marks, like this: a, â, ê, ô, ơ, ư. These diacritical marks are part of the letter and have nothing to do with word accent or tone quality.

The vowels are pronounced:

a—"ah" (long) as in pod
ă—"ah" (short) as in pot
â—"uh" as in but
e—"aa" as in pat
ê—"eh" as in pet
i/y—"ee" as in Pete
o—"aw" as in law

ô—"owe" as in low

ơ—"uh" as in bud

u—"oo" as in coo

ư—"u" as in "ugh"

Of the consonants, only the "d" has two forms. "D" with a line or bar drawn through it (Đ or đ) is pronounced like the English "d." The one without a line or bar is pronounced like our "z" in the north, and like a "y" in central and southern Viet-Nam. The president's name, properly written, has both "d's"—Ngô đinh Diêm. The first is pronounced like our "d"; the second like a "z" or a "y" depending on which part of the country the speaker comes from.

Speaking Vietnamese

There is considerable difference between the way Vietnamese is spoken in various parts of the country. If you learn the southern accent, you may be able to understand people from the north but not necessarily those from central Viet-Nam. Vietnamese in the central provinces of Thanh Hoa and Nghe An have an accent that even their fellow countrymen from other districts find difficult to understand. Huế, too, has its own geographically limited but highly specialized accent.

The sounds of many Vietnamese letters and letter combinations are familiar to English speaking people but a few others are quite difficult to learn, especially the initial "ng" and the vowel "u." To learn to make the "ng" sound, repeat our word "sing" several times, gradually dropping first the "s" and then the "si." To learn to pronounce the Vietnamese "u," say "you" and then broaden the lips as though about to smile, but without moving the position of the tongue.

An advantage of Vietnamese is that once you have learned the sound indicated by a given combination of letters, you know it wherever it appears.

Words beginning with "t" and "th" are pronounced alike except that there is an aspirated (*or* h) sound after the "t" in the "th." The same is true of words spelled with an initial "c" or "k" as compared with the aspirated "ch" or "kh." The importance of knowing how to make this small but tricky distinction is plain when you understand how greatly it changes the meaning of a word. *Tam* means three: *tham*, greedy. *Cam* is orange: *kham*, to suffer.

An "s" and "x" are both pronounced like the "s" in "soap" in northern dialect. But with a southern accent the "s" becomes "sh" as in "shot."

"Nh" is pronounced like the "ny" in "banyan."

Tones Change Meaning

Vietnamese is a monosyllabic language. Each syllable expresses a distinct idea and therefore is a word in itself.

Often two or more syllables are joined to form new words, as in place names like Sai-gon and Ha-noi.

Vietnamese is also tonal. In other words, the tone or level of your voice changes the meaning of a word. The word *ma*, for instance, has many different meanings depending on how you say it, and symbols are used to show the differences.

Word	Symbol	Tone	Meaning
ma	none	level or middle	ghost; to rub
má	´	high	mother; cheek
mà	`	low	but; that; which
mả	?	waving or rising	clever; tomb
mã	~	interrupted	house; appearance
mạ	.	heavy	rice seedling

The northern dialect has these six tones. The southern combines the waving and interrupted tones by pronouncing them in the same way and thus has only five tones. With one exception, tone symbols are placed above the principal vowel of the syllable. The heavy symbol (.) is placed under the principal vowel.

Here's how to use the different tones when talking:

Level tone is a monotone in the middle of the normal speaking range.

The high or high-rising tone starts above level tone and rises sharply.

The low-falling tone starts off in fairly low voice and falls rather slowly to the bottom of the normal range.

The waving or mid-rising tone starts at about level tone, dips very slightly, and then rises slowly.

The interrupted, or high-broken tone starts a bit above normal range, dips a little and then rises abruptly. During the rise the throat is constricted to cause a light, brief interruption of sound.

The heavy or low-dipped tone starts below the middle of the normal speaking range and very abruptly falls. At this point an additional sound is produced by forcing air through the almost closed vocal cords.

Learn by Listening

You can't learn a foreign language, especially a tonal one like Vietnamese, from books alone. You learn it by listening to the way people around you talk and by speaking it yourself. Get a Vietnamese friend or someone else who knows the language well to give you lessons. Getting a good working command of Vietnamese is not easy, but the effort will reward you with a sense of accomplishment and a new feeling of confidence. Too, your ability to speak their language will win the respect of the Vietnamese people with whom you are associated.

USEFUL PHRASES

The word "you" varies in Vietnamese depending on the speaker and the person spoken to. The form used throughout this language guide is *ong*, but it means "you" only when addressing a man. Depending on the person you are addressing, you should replace *ong* with one of the following forms:

married woman	bà
unmarried girl	cô
child (either boy or girl); girl friend; wife	em
close male friend; male servant	anh
female servant	chi

Greetings and Courtesy Phrases

Hello; Goodbye; Good morning; Good afternoon; Goodnight.	Chào ông.
How are you?	Ông mạnh giỏi chớ?
I'm fine.	Tôi mạnh như thường.
I'm glad to meet you.	Tôi hân hạnh được gặp ông.
Please come in and sit down.	Mời ông vào ngồi chơi.

Thank you.	Cám ơn ông.
Don't mention it; It's nothing at all.	Không có gì.
Please speak a little more slowly.	Xin lỗi ông, tôi không hiểu.
Please say it again.	Xin ông nói lại.
Do you speak English?	Ông nói tiếng Anh được không?
No I don't.	Tôi nói không được.
Can you understand me?	Ông hiểu tôi được không?
Yes, I can.	Hiểu được.

Questions and Answers

Most of the following phrases represent highly idiomatic southern Vietnamese. You can compile your own list of nouns by asking the first question and getting the names of things you will most often need to know.

What is this?	Cái này là cái gì?
It's a mango.	Cái này là trái xoài.
Which one?	Cái nào?
Either one.	Cái nào cũng được.
Who's there?	Ai đó?
It's me.	Tôi đây.
It's only me.	Chỉ có một mình tôi.
What does it mean?	Nghĩa là gì?
It has no meaning at all.	Không có nghĩa gì hết.
What kind of person is he?	Ông ấy là người thế nào?

He's a good man.	Ông ấy là người tốt.
How do you work it?	
How do you do it?	Làm thế nào?
Any way.	Thế nào cung được.
This way.	Thế này.
What else?	Còn gì nưã?
All finished; nothing else.	Hết rồi.
Who else?	Còn ai nưã?
You too.	Cũng có ông nưã.
What for?	Để làm gì?
Isn't that so?	Có phải không ông?
That's right.	Phải.
So I've heard.	Tôi có nghe nói như vậy.
Maybe.	Cò lẽ.
I think so.	Tôi nghĩ như vậy.
I guess so.	Tôi đóan như thế.
What's the matter?	Chuyện gì vậy?
Nothing at all.	Không có chuyện gì hết.
I changed my mind.	Tôi đã đổi ý rồi.
I want to ask you a favor.	Tôi muốn phiền ông.
Dinner's ready.	Cơm dọn rồi.
You called the wrong	
number.	Ông gội lầm số.
What's new?	Có gì lạ không?
Nothing's new.	Không có gì lạ.
Who told you?	Ai nói với ông?
You yourself did.	Chính ông nói.

Miscellaneous Phrases

Let's go.	Đi thi đi.
Go away!	Đi đi.
Hurry up!	Mâu lên.
I'm just looking.	Tôi xem chơi.
That's fine; That's enough; I'll take it; Agreed.	Được rồi.

Quantity and Degree

How much is it?	Bao nhiêu tiền?
Not much.	Không bao nhiêu.
Only five *dong*.	Năm đồng thôi.
Five *dong* is too expensive	Năm đồng mắt lám ông ạ.
I'll give you three dong for it.	Tôi trả ba đồng thôi.
They sell all kinds of fruit here.	Ở đây có bán đủ thứ trái cây.
I don't like to eat fruit at all.	Tôi đâu có thích ăn trái cây cã.

Time

What time is it?	Mấy giờ rồi ông?
It's four o'clock.	Bấn giờ rồi.
When did that happen?	Việc ấy xãy ra hồi nào?
Half a month ago.	Cách đây nữa tháng.
August of last year.	Trong tháng tám năm rồi.
When are you going?	Chừng nào ông đi?
In a while.	Một láu nữa.

In a short while.	Không bao lâu nữa.
Soon.	Ít ngay nữa.
Right now.	Bây giờ đây.
Which time?	Lần nào?
Last time.	Lần chót.
The first time.	Lần đầu tiên.
Next time.	Lần tới.
Do you go there often?	Ông đi đến đó thường không?
From time to time.	Thỉnh thoảng thôi.
Every afternoon.	Mỗi bũổi chiều.
Whenever I can.	Lúc nào có dịp.
How long ago?	Được bao lâu rồi?
A long time ago.	Đã lâu rồi.
A while ago.	Hồi nãy.
Too long a time.	Lâu qúa.
The other day.	Hôm nọ.

Location

Where do you live?	Ông ở đâu?
I live in Da Nang.	Tôi ở Đà Nẵng.
Where did you just come from?	Ông ở đâu tới?
I came from Saigon.	Tôi ở Saigon ra.
Where do you come from?	Ông là ngừời ở đâu?
I come from America.	Tôi là ngừời Mỹ.
Where are you going?	Ông đi đâu?
I'm going to the movies.	Tôi đi coi hát bóng.

I'm going home.	Tôi về nhà.
Where have you been?	Ông đi đâu về?
I'm on my way back from the market.	Tôi đi chợ về.
Where is it?	Ở đâu?
Upstairs.	Ở trên lầu.
Downstairs.	Ở dưới nhà.
Inside the house.	Ở trong nhà.
Outside.	Ở ngòai.
Over this way.	Ở đằng này.
Over that way.	Ở đằng đó.
Way over there.	Ở đằng kia kìa.

Military

general	đại tướng
lieutenant general	trung tướng
brigadier general or major general	thiếu tướng
colonel	đai tá
lieutenant colonel	trung tá
major	thiếu tá
captain	dại úy
1st lieutenant	trung úy
2nd lieutenant	thiếu úy
soldier	người lính
sailor	thủy thủ
airman	lính không quân

Days of the Week

Monday	Thứ hai
Tuesday	Thứ ba
Wednesday	Thứ tư
Thursday	Thứ năm
Friday	Thứ sáu
Saturday	Thứ bảy
Sunday	Chủ nhật
today	hôm nay
tomorrow	ngày mai
yesterday	hôm gua

Numbers

1	môt	8	tám
2	hai	9	chín
3	ba	10	mười
4	bốn	20	hai mười
5	năm	25	hai mười lăm
6	sáu	100	một trăm
7	bảy		

THE SECRETARY OF DEFENSE
Washington

5 April 1966

A POCKET GUIDE TO VIETNAM (DoD PG–21A)—This official Department of Defense publication is for the use of personnel in the military Services.

By the Order of the Secretaries of the Army, the Navy, and the Air Force:

HAROLD K. JOHNSON,
General, United States Army,
Chief of Staff.

Official:
J. C. LAMBERT,
Major General, United States
   Army,
The Adjutant General.

B. J. SEMMES, Jr.,
Vice Admiral, United States Navy,
Chief of Naval Personnel.

J. P. McCONNELL,
General U.S. Air Force,
Chief of Staff.

Official:
R. J. PUGH, *Colonel, USAF,*
Director of Administrative
   Services.

H. W. BUSE, Jr.,
Lt. General, U. S. Marine Corps,
Deputy Chief of Staff
(Plans and Programs).

Distribution:
   Army:
      Active Army;
'   Instls (5)
         CINFO, ATTN: Command Information Div. (50)
      NG: None.
      USAR: None.
   Air Force: S (as AFPs 34 series)

SOME DO'S AND DON'TS IN SOUTH VIETNAM

Do be courteous, respectful, and friendly;
Don't be overly familiar with the Vietnamese.

Do learn and respect Vietnamese customs;
Don't forget you are the foreigner.

Do be patient with the Vietnamese attitude toward time;
Don't expect absolute punctuality.

Do appreciate what the South Vietnamese have endured;
Don't give the impression the U. S. is running the war.

Do learn some useful Vietnamese phrases;
Don't expect all Vietnamese to understand English.

Do be helpful when you can;
Don't insist on the Vietnamese doing things your way.

Do learn what the South Vietnamese have to teach;
Don't think Americans know everything.

NAVY UNIFORMS OF VIETNAM

OFFICERS

CAP INSIGNIA

ADMIRAL OF THE FLEET

ADMIRAL

VICE ADMIRAL

REAR ADMIRAL

COMMODO

CAPTAIN

COMMANDER

LIEUTENANT COMMANDER

MARINE INFANTRY INSIGNIA

LIEUTENANT

LIEUTENANT JUNIOR GRADE

ENSIGN

ASPIRANT

LIEUTENANT COMMANDER

OTHER NAVY RANKS

CHIEF WARRANT OFFICER

WARRANT OFFICER

PETTY OFFICER FIRST CLASS

PETTY OFFICER FIRST CLASS

PETTY OFFICER SECOND CLASS

LEADING SEAMAN

SPECIALIS

LEADING SEAM

ABLE SEAMA

SEAMAN